Lawrence Durrell

by G. S. FRASER

Published for the British Council
by Longman Group Ltd

Four shillings net (20p)

Lawrence Durrell's international fame is based on *The Alexandria Quartet* novels, *Justine, Balthazar, Mountolive,* and *Clea,* but this many-sided writer had already acquired a considerable reputation as a poet with the collection *A Private Country* (1943), and as the author of three travel books about Greek islands, *Prospero's Cell* (1945), *Reflections on a Marine Venus* (1953) and *Bitter Lemons* (1957)—the last about his experience in Cyprus during the period of civil strife. He is also the author of three verse plays, of which *An Irish Faustus* (1963) was particularly successful in Germany.

In this essay, G. S. Fraser examines Durrell's work in its different forms and weighs up their respective merits. For some critics it is in the poems and the travel books that Durrell really fulfils himself but Fraser, though finding a special personal intimacy in these, thinks that Durrell's world reputation rightly rests on his fiction. He assesses the significance of an early novel *The Black Book* (1938) as a forerunner of Durrell's individual style and philosophical approach, before going on to examine in close detail *The Alexandria Quartet* and the two latest novels, which form a 'double-decker', *Tunc* (1968) and its sequel *Nunquam* (1970). Fraser praises Durrell's great comic gifts, his skill in plot construction, his rich and ornate prose style, and his ability to create characters that are larger than life. He concludes: 'Quite apart from the permanent value of his best writing . . . [Durrell] holds out a valuable lesson, an exemplary lesson to the younger writers of today. He has never stopped trying and learning.'

Reader in Modern English Literature at the University of Leicester, born in Scotland, G. S. Fraser is a poet, critic, and teacher who has taught English in Japan and, more recently, in the United States. His most recent volume of poems is *Conditions* (1969). One volume of literary history *The Modern Writer and His World* was first published in Japan in 1951 and, under various imprints and with various publishers, has been continuously in print since then, with periodical revisions. An edition with a new epilogue came out in 1970. His monograph *Ezra Pound* (1960) has been translated into French and Spanish. His most recent prose book is a technical study, *Metre, Rhyme, and Free Verse* (1970). A longer essay on his present subject, *Lawrence Durrell: A Study,* came out in 1968. He is the author of *W. B. Yeats* and *Dylan Thomas* in the present series.

LAWRENCE DURRELL

by

G. S. Fraser

Edited by Ian Scott-Kilvert

Mark Gerson

LAWRENCE DURRELL

LAWRENCE DURRELL

by

G. S. FRASER

PUBLISHED FOR
THE BRITISH COUNCIL
BY LONGMAN GROUP LTD

LONGMAN GROUP LTD
Longman House, Burnt Mill, Harlow, Essex

*Associated companies, branches and
representatives throughout the world*

First published 1970
© G. S. Fraser 1970

*Printed in Great Britain by
F. Mildner & Sons, London, EC1*

CONTENTS

I. THE CAREER, THE REPUTATION   7

II. THE POEMS   16

III. ISLANDS   24

IV. THE BLACK BOOK:
A SPIRITUAL AUTOBIOGRAPHY   27

V. THE ALEXANDRIA QUARTET   33

VI. *TUNC* AND *NUNQUAM*   39

A SELECT BIBLIOGRAPHY   45

LAWRENCE DURRELL

I. THE CAREER, THE REPUTATION

LAWRENCE GEORGE DURRELL was born in 1912 in India, of which there are a few glimpses, as seen from childhood memory, in his first and least successful novel, *Pied Piper of Lovers* (1935). In his early teens, his family returned to England, settling in Bournemouth, and he went to school in England, began to write poems in his late teens and novels in his early twenties, mingling in the early 1930s with London literary Bohemia and, rather later, in Paris with writers such as Anaïs Nin and Henry Miller, the latter of whom had a great moral influence on him.

Though Durrell was very young when he began to write, publishing privately his first pamphlet of poems at nineteen, he did not begin to make a significant reputation as a poet till 1943, when he was thirty-one, with the volume *A Private Country*. In 1935, on his advice, his family (his mother, one sister, two brothers, one of whom, Gerald, was also to become well known as a writer) transferred itself from Bournemouth to Corfu. *Pied Piper of Lovers* was followed a little later in the 1930s by a more competent but still basically conventional novel, *Panic Spring*, published under the pseudonym Charles Norden. Durrell's first really original prose work, a semi-autobiographical fantasia called *The Black Book*, was published in 1938 in Paris: it has since been published in the USA, but not in England where it thus enjoys an underground reputation: it has, however, been republished in America.

Durrell, with his first wife Nancy, was living in Corfu in the years just before the Second World War. He kept a full diary and took many notes about the flora, fauna, history, and human characters of the island, which he worked up in 1945 into the first of his three island books, *Prospero's Cell*. After leaving Corfu, he taught for a while

7

in southern Greece, escaped with his wife in a caïque to
Alexandria from the Axis invaders, and in Egypt during the
war, after a short period of free-lance journalism, served in
Cairo and Alexandria in various official posts as Press
Officer and Information Officer. In 1945 and 1946, he was
Press Officer for the Allied Government in Rhodes, and
accumulated material for his second island book, *Reflections
on a Marine Venus*, which did not, however, get published
till 1953. The poems and the travel books were earning
Durrell a distinguished if not quite a major reputation, but
he could not live on his writing.

He had children to support both by his first wife Nancy,
who had parted from him in Egypt, and his second wife,
Eve, whom he had met there. The period in Rhodes was
followed by a spell as a lecturer for the British Council in
Argentina, which he disliked, and a period as Press Attaché
with the British Embassy in Yugoslavia. He was not happy
there either; his second marriage began to break up, and
in 1952 he went with his small daughter to Cyprus,
determined at last to embark on the ambitious novel about
Alexandria about which he had brooded for many years.

With his savings, he bought a small Turkish house in a
village, and supplemented his income by teaching English
in a Cypriot grammar school. With the outbreak of the
troubles, however, his official services were again called
upon. He felt a bitter conflict between his fondness for the
Cypriot and his loyalty to Great Britain, and in the autumn
of 1956 came to England where, in a cottage borrowed from
a friend in Dorset, he completed *Justine* and wrote, much
more rapidly than he had written his other island books,
Bitter Lemons, based on his experiences in Cyprus.

Both books were, for the first time in Durrell's career as
a writer, notable popular as well as critical successes. He has
had very marked success in his literary career, but he has
always had to wait for it. His first volume of poems was
published twelve years after his first teenage pamphlet of
poems. The great success of *Justine* came in 1957 twenty-two

years after the complete failure, financially and critically, of *Pied Piper of Lovers*, published in 1935. Durrell was in his early thirties when he attained a real reputation as a poet, in his forty-fourth year when he acquired world-wide fame as a novelist.

The success of *Justine* enabled Durrell for the first time in his life to devote all his energies to writing. He settled in the south of France with a married woman, Claude, whom he had met in Cyprus, and who obtained a divorce and was able to marry him in 1961; she died in 1965. The two immediate successors to *Justine*, *Balthazar* and *Mountolive*, written rapidly but with verve (Durrell can work fourteen hours a day at the typewriter), were both published in 1958. The coda to *The Alexandria Quartet*, *Clea*, was a shorter book, and therefore, on a principle expressed by Pascal in *The Provincial Letters*, took longer to write. It came out in 1960. In 1962, all four novels, with numerous revisions and a new preface, were published in one volume as *The Alexandria Quartet*.

They have been translated into most European languages, are also widely read in the United States and in the Far and Farther East, and, next to Graham Greene, Durrell perhaps now enjoys a wider world-fame than any other English novelist. Durrell feels that he can only attempt major works in fiction at considerable intervals. He is a good professional, and must always be writing something, and 1957, the year of *Justine* and *Bitter Lemons*, also saw the publication of a John Buchanesque thriller, *White Eagles Over Serbia*, and a book of Wodehousian farcical short stories about Embassy life in the Balkans, *Esprit de Corps*; this has had several sequels. Such books might be described as honest and un-patronizing pot-boilers; an omnivorous reader of popular fiction in his boyhood, Durrell puts into such books a still boyish zest. He is, as a person and a writer, an admirable exemplification of the maxim of the great Chinese moral philosopher Mencius, that a mandarin ought always to retain a touch of the boy in himself.

The one *genre* of writing in which Durrell, not pot-boiling, but taking himself very seriously indeed, has not achieved either popular or critical success, is the verse play. His first verse play, *Sappho*, was published in 1950, but not, though there was a Third Programme broadcast of it, publicly performed in Great Britain till the Edinburgh Festival of 1961. This performance coincided with the renaissance of English prose drama associated with the names of John Osborne, of Samuel Beckett, of Harold Pinter, and with the vogue for Brecht in translation. Though full of beautiful passages of lyrical and meditative verse, it perhaps lacks the tensions and confrontations that are proper to drama; it is more like a versification of one of Landor's *Imaginary Conversations*. In his next verse play, *Acte*, Durrell took this lesson to heart, and it is a melodrama in the style of Corneille, about honour and self-sacrifice, in which the language (the play was first produced in Germany, and in his published version Durrell has respected the German producer's cuts) is noticeably more rhetorical than is usual in Durrell's verse.

The best of Durrell's verse plays seems to me to be *An Irish Faustus*, a morality play in nine scenes, alternately farcical and frightening. His Faustus is somewhat reminiscent of Prospero, a magician who throws away his wand. In translation this play has proved a considerable success in the German theatre. Most great playwrights from Shakespeare to Ibsen have been actively involved in what Yeats called 'theatre business, management of men'. I think that Durrell's verse plays, like those of Wordsworth, Keats, Shelley, Browning, Tennyson, have suffered from his thinking of the verse play as primarily *literature*: he has never thought much of the problems of production, of timing, of the control of the audience, that 'great beast'.

I cannot imagine any of Durrell's plays having a success in the contemporary English theatre. They might have a better chance in Ireland, for example at the Abbey Theatre in Dublin or at the annual Yeats Festival in Sligo, in a culture which accepts lyricism, dance, on the stage, and does not demand naturalism or topicality at any cost. I respect the integrity and unworldliness of Durrell's dramatic efforts more, I think, than most critics have done. If he had started writing verse plays five years earlier, he might have had a similar sort of success, in the late 1940s and early 1950s, to that of T. S. Eliot, Christopher Fry, and Ronald Duncan. Yet even in that period his lack of intimate knowledge of stage technique might have proved a handicap; so might his self-imposed exile from the ever-changing idioms, pitches, informalities, of spoken English.

In 1968, Durrell published the first part of a two-decker novel *Aut Tunc Aut Nunquam*[1], which puzzled and distressed most English critics, though a fine fellow-professional, Angus Wilson, noted Durrell's skill in contriving plot and controlling the pace of narrative. The characters, as Durrell himself noticed, were more 'puppets' than those in *The Alexandria Quartet*, the scenic backgrounds more perfunctory. Most reviewers (including myself) could not make out exactly what he meant by saying that whereas *The Alexandria Quartet* was mainly about 'religion', *Tunc*, and its sequel *Nunquam* (published in 1970) were mainly about 'culture': in a letter to a friend at the end of *Nunquam* Durrell makes it clear that he had in mind Spengler's distinction between organically complete cultures, going through the natural stages of spring, summer, autumn, winter, and the long winter between the death of an old culture and the birth of a new, what Spengler distinguished from 'culture' as 'civilization'. There are analogies to these ideas in, for instance, Arnold Toynbee's *A Study of History* and Yeats's *A Vision*. I shall deal with these two ambitious and entertaining books of Durrell's at the end of this pamphlet.

Durrell's reputation in Europe, Asia, and America rests mainly on *The Alexandria Quartet*; his reputation in England

---

[1] These four words ('either then or never') represent a quotation from Petronius which inspired the titles of the two separate volumes: these have been published separately as *Tunc* and *Nunquam*.

rests rather more, I think, on his poetry and his travel-books, though there are many critics who feel that *The Alexandria Quartet* is a most impressive but in some ways flawed or imperfect work, extraordinarily vivid, but too rich, too gaudy.

I have taken the shorter works in passing; in the rest of this pamphlet, I shall deal in turn with the poems, with Durrell's first really original prose-work, *The Black Book*, with *The Alexandria Quartet*, and with the *Tunc-Nunquam* double-decker. It was his poems which, when I first came across them in a little magazine, Nicholas Moore's *Seven*, in 1938, first attracted me to Durrell. I still feel that he is perhaps most naturally himself in his poems, and in his books about islands, though clearly more vigorous and ambitious in his attempts at major prose fiction.

Something should be said, at the end of the introductory section of this pamphlet, about the marked contrast between Durrell's European, American and Asian reputation and his present reputation at home. It might be said that he has the virtues and vices of a tuppence-coloured writer during a British post-war period, at first of great austerity, and later of quiet but fundamental social change, a period in which much of the best British writing has been penny-plain. In a period of good 'drab' writing, in C. S. Lewis's sense, he has attempted the 'golden' style. As a young man he would have liked to go to Cambridge (or so I have been told, though he has not personally confirmed this to me), and one wonders what would have happened to him if he had read English for three years at Downing College under Dr Leavis.

Durrell has a special admiration for Kipling, Thackeray, and Surtees, three fine writers who fall very much outside Dr Leavis's 'great tradition'. His earliest really original prose work, *The Black Book*, is full of affectionate parodies of great English writers in what George Saintsbury called the 'ornate' style: Pater, Landor, De Quincey. His art, in prose, is never or rarely—for he can, from time to time, write a very plain narrative prose, as in his early 'situation' novel, *Cefalû* (1945), or in some of the more straightforward sections of *Mountolive*—an art that conceals art. He likes impasto, bravura effects, firework set-pieces. He has a certain taste for the gaudy and for the richly improbable.

Durrell knows, perhaps, comparatively little about contemporary England, though he is a very shrewd observer of the rich eccentric burgeonings of the English character, transferred to a hot climate. To know what has been happening in the changing social structure of England over the past forty years one would not turn to Durrell (except perhaps to the very early Durrell of *The Black Book*) but, say, to Anthony Powell for in-group comedy, Angus Wilson for a broad Dickensian handling of social hypocrisies and pretences (and a similarly Dickensian warmth towards humble decencies), and C. P. Snow for a study of government by committee. In a broad sense, all these are 'realistic': or perhaps Wilson, an admirer of Zola, and a great piler-up of sometimes superfluous 'documentary' detail, might be called a 'naturalistic' writer.

In Durrell, fiction is consciously fictive; it is always transforming itself from the transcription of what life is like to an attempt to create the myth, myth rather than allegory, of what life is. Perhaps the home-keeping writer whom Durrell most resembles is Iris Murdoch, who, like Durrell, enjoys playing (almost as in a logical game with truth-tables) with the permutations and combinations of possible sexual relationships, who enjoys both the violent and the improbable, and who likes to show sexual and religious drives improbably and grotesquely fusing. Like Durrell, Miss Murdoch writes what might be called philosophical fables, and like Durrell she does not disdain the tall story or the purple patch. Like Durrell, she has, in England, a very wobbly critical reputation; there are those who would describe both of them as brilliant frauds. Both, perhaps, as prose-writers, are in the tradition of something that we might call romance or fantasy rather than in the tradition of the 'straight' novel. But this *genre* has its own distinction and validity.

An acute reviewer of *Nunquam*, Christopher Holmes, noticed that this most recent major effort of Durrell's cannot, unlike *The Alexandria Quartet*, be sensibly compared, say, with Proust. The relevant models or analogues are philosophic romances of the romantic period like Mary Shelley's *Frankenstein* or William Godwin's *Caleb Williams*. In *Tunc* and *Nunquam*, Durrell for the first time takes the risk of appealing *simultaneously* to what might be called his pop audience, the audience for the Antrobus stories, the 'situation' novel *Cefalû* (later retitled *The Dark Labyrinth*), *White Eagles over Serbia*, and the sophisticated audience which welcomed the island books and the poems and, if less certain about *The Alexandria Quartet*, saw this at least as a nobly ambitious effort in a great tradition, perhaps (to use the phrase of an old acquaintance of Durrell's to me) 'a flawed masterpiece, but not fatally flawed'.

I attended a press conference given by Durrell before the publication of *Nunquam*, at which he made a number of critically interesting remarks. Over the last ten years or so, he has had a growing interest in the macabre and the shocking. He feels that literature must now compete for attention with the instant thrills and horrors of contemporary history, newspaper headlines, posters, television programmes, and therefore must make an almost brutally direct impact on the reader. He mentioned Edgar Allan Poe who combines a taste for the grotesque and macabre with a taste for cosmological philosophizing. Durrell said, in a striking phrase, that he aimed in *Tunc* and *Nunquam*, at being 'horrid' without being 'nasty'. (What one finds nasty, of course, is a subjective matter; it depends on one's high or low threshold of squeamishness.)

In one sense, *Tunc* and *Nunquam* might be thought to belong to the same family as Aldous Huxley's *Brave New World* and George Orwell's *1984*. But there is a deep difference. Durrell's temperament is a buoyant and sanguine, in a sense an optimistic temperament. Durrell believes profoundly, in a Kierkegaardian sense, in man's freedom, his ability at any and every moment to take Kierkegaard's leap in the dark, away from the unauthentic or conformist life. We are living, he feels, in a technocratic period of ruthless organization, crushing and channelling of individual lives. But it is no good for the individual to seek freedom merely for himself. None of us is free (and, though Durrell's political instincts are profoundly conservative, this is an oddly Marxist observation) unless all of us are free; unless the organizations that control us become themselves imbued with the spirit of freedom.

Durrell discussed these ideas in a film presented on the BBC's Number Two television programme in relation to a Provençal tramp called Blanco, a house-painter, who at the age of 35 suddenly flung down his brush, and began wandering about the roads of Provence, throwing his hat ahead of himself in the early morning and following, across fields, through woods, in whatever direction it led (a kind of modern equivalent, except that Blanco was no scholar, of Arnold's Scholar Gypsy). Durrell spoke in this programme of how he felt himself tied down by possessions, two houses in Provence, one with a swimming pool: how in a sense he envied Blanco.

The pretty young Frenchwoman who acted as Durrell's interlocutor, stooge, or 'straight man', pointed out to Durrell that sleeping alone like a tramp is very sad. Though cheap wine is easily available in the South of France, even for tramps, one cannot go to bed with a bottle. Durrell agreed with her. But the film expressed something very deep in Durrell, the wish not to be tied down, the recurrent need for a fresh start, the impulse of the wanderer. It also conveyed, as I think his writing conveys, something which literary criticism can hardly deal with: Durrell's extraordinary openness as a person, his vulnerability (though he is not a touchy or a hard person), his freshness. Any striking thing that anybody said to Durrell at any time might be

like the directional throwing forward of the tramp Blanco's
bashed old hat.

II. THE POEMS

Francis Hope, in a sparkling though scathing review of my
longer monograph on Durrell (*Lawrence Durrell: A Study*,
1968), referred to the poems and the travel books as Durrell's
most permanent achievements. I shall deal with the poems
first because when I first came across them in two important
little magazines, Nicholas Moore's *Seven* and Tambimuttu's
Poetry London, in the late 1930s, these were what 'hooked'
me on Durrell as a new and unknown writer of wholly
individual talent, 'a new voice in a new time'.

The poems are still, it seems to me, the part of his writings
where Durrell is most his natural self. In the 1930s, a period
of much polemical political verse, these poems did not
harangue. Compared, also, with the prose of *The Black Book*,
of which Nicholas Moore published some samples in *Seven*,
they did not strike me as too highly coloured, congested,
over-spiced. Durrell's poems have from their beginnings
been beautifully modulated; by the word 'modulation' I
mean the way in which a really skilful poet can move gently
from the expression of one mood at the beginning of a poem
to that of a contrasting, contrary, or more fully inclusive
mood at the end of a poem, without any effect like that of a
motor-car abruptly and crashingly changing gears. Modulation in this sense is closely related to what I. A. Richards
calls 'tone', a poet's tact in anticipating and handling the
responses of his imagined audience.

Durrell's tone in poetry I would call one of quiet amenity,
of controlled poignancy. (A witty but rather malicious critic
once said to me that in his poetry Durrell has taste without
genius, in his prose genius without taste.) The poetic
personality that came across to me when I read those early
poems which appeared so fugitively in the 1930s was one

gentle, compassionate, temperamentally sad but quirkily humorous, essentially lonely. I thought these early poems also (as I think the later poems) the work of a religiously-minded man.

This is not to say that Durrell is poetically concerned with religious dogmas or with crisis-states, such as those which may precede conversion. He is concerned with the expression of an interior religious mood that one might call quietism or, in Gabriel Marcel's term, *recueillement*, self-recollection, the ingathering of the self with all it reflects upon itself: concerned with an often sad, but always grateful and affectionate cosmic piety. If Durrell is a kind of mystic he is the kind of mystic who is concerned more with the All than the One. The single fierce God of Semitic religion is not invoked in his poems, only the *genius loci*, the little god of the particular landscape. Yet though he is concerned both in poetry and prose with the plurality, the multifariousness, the plenitude of life, he is concerned with these also as manifestations of some ground or process which is ultimately single.

The early poems, like the later poems, were self-communings, but there was nothing excessively or rawly private, like some of the passages, for instance, in Auden or Eliot. The two poets whom Durrell most admired at the beginning of his poetic career *were* Auden and Eliot. In his preoccupation with landscape and historical sites, and their emblematic human meanings, he still has close affinities with Auden; like Auden he thinks of human roles and characters as largely a function of human ecology. Like Auden, he was much struck in youth both with the psychology of Groddeck, who sees physical illness and neurotic behaviour as an expression of the thwarting of the It (not Freud's Id, but a predetermined and unconscious seed of the life-pattern) and with Kretschmer's close relating of human temperament to physique. He thinks of himself as, in Kretschmer's terminology, a pyknic—round, short, bouncy, muscular, socially extroverted, capable of creating instant social fun.

One can see some of Auden's tricks and devices in Durrell even today. The influence of Eliot is harder to trace. Eliot, for every great new poem, each 'stage on life's way' (Kierkegaard's phrase), created an essentially new style, though hoarding and using again and again with frugal prodigality a few obsessional key images: fogs, streets, corners, cats of various kinds, lilacs, hyacinths, eyes, gardens. Eliot's influence on his younger contemporaries is pervasive but, as Auden has said, hard to trace in good poets in the detail of their work. Perhaps Eliot's greatest influence on Durrell was not on Durrell's verse, but on his strange early prose work, his first really original book, *The Black Book*, which could be considered as a kind of expanded prose variation of *The Waste Land*.

Durrell has never lost his freshness as a poet, but I do not think one can speak of his *development*, as one speaks of development in Eliot, Yeats, or Auden. As a writer both in prose and verse, I think Durrell acquired what educational psychologists call a 'set', a framework for perceiving the world, probably in mid-adolescence. All his writing from the age of nineteen or twenty onwards has been a feeding of experience into the 'set' rather than a use of experience fundamentally to change it. Clearly, it was a good or useful 'set', but one has always a sense, as it were, of Durrell durrellizing experience rather than of experience un-durrellizing Durrell. I think this makes him a very good minor rather than a major poet. Most major poets have faced at some stage what Scott Fitzgerald called 'the crack-up', and have magnificently stood up, brushed off the broken bits of coloured glass—I am thinking of the Claude-glass, by which landscape painters of the eighteenth century could turn the raw green of real grass and leaves into a 'mellow brown' appropriate to traditional convention —and started doing something quite new.

I am not sure that Durrell, even in his more adventurous excursions in prose, *The Black Book*, *The Alexandria Quartet*, and *Tunc* and *Nunquam*, ever got rid of the Claude-glass.

He differs from his friend the American writer, Henry Miller, who has been a great influence on him, in that literature for him is always something done with words, not something that gets beyond words. He differs from Miller, also, in being fundamentally a reticent and reserved writer, about his private life. His correspondence with Miller, edited by George Weekes, is, in what has been printed, essentially a 'literary' correspondence, a technical one: a correspondence about the ideas and problems of the writer *as* writer. And the 'I' of the three island books, *Prospero's Cell*, *Reflections on a Marine Venus*, *Bitter Lemons*, is—though least in the last of these, which is a bitter and direct book— an edited version of the author, a small human figure put into a large painted landscape to give scale.

Darley and Pursewarden, of course, in *The Alexandria Quartet* project (and all projection implies a kind of profiled simplification) aspects of Durrell's own experience and character: yet they are frankly fictive, also, in a frankly fictive world. But the poems, in their quiet and urbane modesty combined with confidence, are as near, not to confessional writing, but to what Yeats calls 'heart-revealing intimacy' as, perhaps, Durrell ever gets.

Durrell's poems seem to me to fall into not more than four or five main categories. There are a number of short lyrical poems whose main charm lies in their musicality (as a very young man Durrell tried, not very successfully, to write words and compose tunes for Tin-Pan Alley lyrics). Then there are meditative and descriptive poems, reflections on the spirit of place, history, memories, friendship. There are a number of very pleasant light and comic poems, the equivalent of Robert Graves's 'satires and grotesques'. There are some rather Browningesque poems, appreciations of character, about Horace, La Rochefoucauld, and Byron, for instance, each seen in a different way as examples of the pain and limitation of the artist's life, as well as its achievement. My possible fifth category would be short lyrical poems which are, of course, musical but are more memorable for a riddling metaphysical content than for their musicality. Though these shorter lyrical, musical or metaphysical poems are shaped with great care, there is in the longer poems sometimes a deliberate 'roughening up' of the texture. What looks like carelessness here is not so. There is a line in a fine poem written in Egypt during the war, 'Alexandria':

> Or like a walker in the darkness might . . .

I used to worry very much about what seems, at first, the sub-literate use of 'like' for 'as'. The poet Hilary Corke pointed out to me that the *k* of 'like' locks in with the *k*s of 'walker' and 'darkness' and that the diphthong of 'like' chimes with the diphthong of 'might'.

From his earliest to his latest poems, Durrell has this concern with verbal texture, with sound-sense relationships. One way in which he has perhaps technically developed is in making this concern a little less obtrusive than in his earliest work, in achieving an impression of careless ease. Rather similarly, from *The Black Book* to *The Alexandria Quartet*, and from *The Alexandria Quartet* to *Tunc* and *Nunquam*, the prose is always rich and ornate, but *The Black Book* is congested and self-conscious in a way that *The Alexandria Quartet* is not, and *Tunc* and *Nunquam* move with a kind of ease, the style sometimes spoofing itself or 'sending itself up', in a way that is not typical of the great technicolour blocs, the magnificent set pieces, of *The Alexandria Quartet*. As a prose writer, Durrell has always wanted the reader to say, 'Gosh!' He now says 'Gosh!' himself, in a rather chuckling way.

Let me quote a stanza from the poem 'Alexandria' which I have already mentioned. In this poem, as later in *The Alexandria Quartet*, the city of Alexandria becomes an emblem of, or symbol for, a civilization already in decay and threatened by war, a place of exile, a place where the artist's very loneliness intensifies his sense of the fused richness and tragedy of life: a place of great sensuality, and yet

also of remote and difficult spiritual and artistic aspiration.
Concrete and topical, indeed, as the poem is, it is a lasting
poem, since for all of us in Western Europe our Alexandria
is here and now:

> So we, learning to suffer and not condemn
> Can only wish you this great pure wind
> Condemned by Greece, and turning like a helm,
> Inland where it smokes the fires of men,
> Spins weathercocks on farms or catches
> The lovers at their quarrel in the sheets;
> Or like a walker in the darkness might,
> Knocks and disturbs the artist at his papers
> Up there alone, upon the alps of night.

This stanza might be a better epigraph than various
sentences from that prolix sophist de Sade for *The
Alexandria Quartet*. Most of the scenes and topics of the four
interlinked novels are sketched here; the inland farms, the
lovers at their quarrel in the sheets, the walker in the darkness, the artist's effort and loneliness, the progress of the soul
through learning to suffer and not condemn, and the pure
wind (the wind of the spirit that bloweth where it listeth)
reviving and disturbing lives that have become like stagnant
water.

The poems about artists have also a very close relationship
to the major prose works. *The Black Book* and *The Alexandria Quartet* are, almost like *Trilby* or *La Vie de Bohême*,
about artists, about those who fail to become artists, about
those who, self-destructively, treat their lives as an art-work,
about those, like Pursewarden, who achieve the state of the
true artist but begin again, striving for a state of love or
truth which lies on the other side of possible artistic expression. Perhaps the finest of these poems is 'On First Looking
Into Loeb's Horace'. Durrell adds his own notes to the notes
of a friend whose copy he has borrowed:

> Here, where your clear hand marked up
> 'The hated cypress' I added 'Because it grew
> On tombs, revealing his fear of autumn and the urns',

> Depicting a solitary at an upper window
> Revising metaphors for the winter sea: 'O
> Dark head of storm-tossed curls'; or silently
> Watching the North Star which like a fever burns
>
> Away the envy and neglect of the common,
> Shining on this terrace, lifting up in recreation
> The sad heart of Horace who must have seen it only
> As a metaphor for the self and its perfection ——
> A burning heart quite constant in its station.

An artist (at least in verse) rather like Horace, a very patient reviser of metaphors, Durrell richly conveys here both the splendour and the wretchedness of the artist's vocation. Elsewhere, in the poem, Horace is described as 'fat, lonely, and unloved'. In this passage the phrase 'the envy and neglect of the common' does not, of course, refer to the common people's envy and neglect of a prosperous and great poet, but to the lonely artist's envy of everyday happiness, and his neglect of the common pieties of everyday affection that make happiness possible.

There is great psychological acuteness later on in this poem in the description of Horace's having 'the pose of sufficiency, the landed man'—the artist is usually not quite a gentleman but, if successful, is allowed to pretend that he is one!—and of Horace's

> Disguising a sense of failure in a hatred for the young.

Horace's Sabine farm, and by implication his poetry, are described as this 'forgery/Of completeness'. The word 'forgery' both suggests the craft of the goldsmith or silversmith and the idea of something counterfeit. Neither art in itself, nor the life of the artist, can for Durrell be genuinely complete. There is something beyond art to which art is only a path.

The unevenness of Durrell's writing, his readiness to turn his hand to many sorts of pot-boiling, the occasional slapdash or overwritten passages even in his more ambitious prose, can no doubt partly be ascribed to his often having had to write rapidly and copiously, to earn money, and partly to frank and honest failures of taste, or boyishness of taste: in prose, at least, Durrell nearly always prefers tuppence-coloured to penny-plain. But the unevenness can much more fundamentally be ascribed to a feeling Durrell has that art is generally ranked far too high in the scale of human activities: there are things, as Marianne Moore says, 'beyond all this fiddle'. Durrell often uses words like 'love' or 'feeling' or, more recently, in *Tunc* and *Nunquam*, 'freedom' to express what it is that is more important than art, and his sense of the imprisonment of the mere artist in art. Horace is 'held from loving by a sort of wall'. La Rochefoucauld is made to say, 'I could not get beyond this wall', and also:

> Though love is not the word I want
> Yet it will have to do. There is no other.

I have been treating the poems, perhaps, too much as clues to Durrell's prose writings and his 'philosophy'. To show simply how beautiful they can be, here is a complete short poem, 'Lesbos', expanded from a hint from Sappho:

> The Pleiades are sinking calm as paint,
> The earth's huge camber follows out,
> Turning in sleep, the oceanic curve.
>
> Defined in concave like a human eye
> Or a cheek pressed warm on the dark's cheek,
> Like dancers to a music they deserve.
>
> This balcony, a moon-anointed shelf
> Above a silent garden holds my bed.
> I slept. But the dispiriting autumn moon,
>
> In her slow expurgation of the sky
> Needs company: is brooding on the dead,
> And so am I now, so am I.

This is about cosmic harmony and human love as reciprocal metaphors for each other (which is vehicle, which tenor?) It is about the inevitable loneliness of the artist who is part neither of the love nor the harmony, but the wistful and accurate observer of both. That good old stage property, the moon, makes yet another farewell appearance in poetry, but with a slightly new role, purifying the sky, as the poet must purify his heart. This could be called a perfect short poem—a little too conscious of its perfection, perhaps?—but it moves us because of the yearning, because of the piety towards the dead, and the reminder that perfection, like patriotism, is 'not enough'. Durrell's poems are a series of quiet but insistent reminders that the mixed richness of life, for which he has such a relish, and the possible limited perfection of small works of art, a perfection which in verse though not in prose he can sometimes achieve, are both signposts to something beyond themselves. Taken as the destination both richness of content and finality of form become congested, claustrophobic, indigestible, a wall.

Yet, paradoxically, though Durrell feels this very deeply (and though this is the main thing his poems are, so to say, 'talking about'), the poems themselves remain exceedingly 'enclosed' poems. Durrell does not wrestle violently to 'break out' of his poems, to peck through the shell from within, in the manner, say, of Robert Lowell in *Life Studies* or Sylvia Plath. He is a poet of ordered distance rather than violent immediacy. The poems are not, of course, any more than anybody else's poems, all equally good. Sometimes Durrell relaxes into a kind of stylish doodling. But the graph of achievement is a fairly even wave pattern rather than a jagged series of peaks and valleys. The sustained coherence and consistency of mood, tone, and craftsmanlike care over a poetic career of forty years or so is honourable and impressive. Some critics have seen Durrell in his prose works as a kind of first-rate con man, a brilliant charlatan. In verse, he never bluffs or cheats.

III. ISLANDS

Durrell's three topographical books, *Prospero's Cell* (1945), *Reflections on a Marine Venus* (1953), and *Bitter Lemons* (1957) are about Greek islands. In 1937 and 1938, after the enormous emotional effort of writing his first really original prose work, *The Black Book*, Durrell returned to Corfu, where his mother had earlier rented a house, with his first wife, Nancy. By contrast with *The Black Book*, *Prospero's Cell*, based on these pre-Second World War Corfu years, is pastoral comedy, a landscape with characters: perhaps almost a little too consistently sweet and bland all through. Durrell made copious notes for a book on Corfu in 1938 and 1939, but only reconstituted these towards the end of the Second World War, when he had spent about five years on official service in Egypt, and when Nancy had left him. No retrospective hurt or bitterness, no anticipation of coming violence, clouds his picture of Nancy's doe-like beauty, or of a timeless and crystalline world.

The second travel book, *Reflections on a Marine Venus*, is similarly built up in retrospect from Durrell's experience as an Information Officer in Rhodes in 1945 and 1946. This is not such a smoothly shaped work, it bulges rather at the seams with scraps of miscellaneous information, but it confronts reality with a harder and sadder eye. Durrell went to Rhodes wondering if his picture of Corfu had been a sentimental one, that of a tourist living cheaply because of local poverty and a favourable rate of exchange. He found in Rhodes an island shattered by war and poverty. What struck him now was not an atmosphere of pastoral romance, but the stoical courage of the Greek people. His characters are no longer pastoral comedy characters, but real people who have suffered. There is still much fine description of landscape, much comedy of humours, much bravura writing, but the deep feeling is that life is a hard and bitter, though noble, business.

The third travel book, *Bitter Lemons*, was written not retrospectively but almost journalistically. In 1952 Durrell came to Cyprus with his small daughter by his second marriage which had by then broken up. There, as I have mentioned, his work on *Justine* was interrupted by the outbreak of the Cyprus troubles and Durrell's various and always successful public service career made it inevitable that he should once again be offered official employment— because of his early years in Corfu, and his great natural gift for languages, he spoke fluent modern Greek.

Emotionally, Durrell was deeply torn between his liking for both Greek and Turkish Cypriots, his happiness as a member of a small, friendly village community, and a simple, old-fashioned, perhaps slightly prickly British patriotism: his Kipling side.

Gradually his fellow villagers began to avoid him: his best friend, a Greek schoolmaster, was killed. He felt that strong military action against terrorists was necessary, but also that it made any long-range political settlement between Great Britain and Cyprus impossible. He saw Great Britain as squandering an enormous capital of Hellenic good-will, founded by Lord Byron and renewed in the Second World War, by the comradeship of Greek and Briton as members of the Resistance in Greece and Crete. Sad and disillusioned, he left Cyprus in the autumn of 1956 and borrowed a cottage in Dorset, where he wrote *Bitter Lemons*, his book about his experiences in Cyprus, very rapidly. The prose style is much more plain and direct than in the other two island books, and Durrell's troubled frankness exacts a great deal of sympathy. A Book Society choice, *Bitter Lemons* was Durrell's first big popular success.

Some English critics (the verdict of European and American critics would be quite different) feel that it is in the poems and the island books that Durrell really fulfils himself. The argument of such critics as Francis Hope or John Lehmann is that in *The Black Book*, *The Alexandria Quartet*, and the double-decker *Tunc* and *Nunquam*, Durrell is, in Wallace Stevens's sense, letting the imagination breed incestuously from the imaginary. The ambitious fictions, in this case against them, are too self-indulgent, too grandiose, too much pure fantasia. In the poems, such critics would say, Durrell found a tone, and in the island books not only a tone but a scale, that exactly suited his talents and his personality. I would not agree; I would agree that the more ambitious fictions are vulnerable to critical sniping in a way in which the poems and the island books are not, and that the poems and the island books are the things to read first if one wants to approach Durrell the novelist through a sense of Durrell the man.

IV. THE BLACK BOOK: A SPIRITUAL AUTOBIOGRAPHY

So let us look now at the novels, on which Durrell's world-reputation mainly rests. In an early letter to Henry Miller, some time in the later 1930s, Durrell wrote that his first and simplest literary ambition had been to be a best-selling novelist (an ambition which he has achieved, as we mostly achieve ambitions which we are passionate and single-minded enough about in extreme youth). Durrell's first novel, *Pied Piper of Lovers*, submitted by him for a first-novel competition which it did not win, and his second novel, *Panic Spring*, published under a pseudonym, Charles Norden, because of the critical and commercial failure of his first novel, both novels written by a young man in his early to middle twenties, are interesting only because Durrell wrote them. The first has some good passages based on Durrell's childhood in India; the second, a much more competent piece of writing, was about the sensitive English puritan exposed to the Mediterranean world, in the tradition of Aldous Huxley's *These Barren Leaves* and, more remotely, of Norman Douglas's *South Wind*. It is a weakness of young writers with an excessive passion for literature to try to do again what has already been more or less finally done. Smoothly and elegantly written, *Panic Spring* lacked inner springiness.

The publishers of *Panic Spring*, Faber and Faber, seeing perhaps in Durrell a reliable if not exciting upper-middlebrow talent, gave him a contract for two or three more novels. But his third work of fiction (it is more an auto-biographical fantasia than a novel proper), *The Black Book*, astonished them. It was inspired both in its freedom of form and its erotic frankness by Henry Miller's *Tropic of Cancer*. T. S. Eliot admired it very much, and Faber were willing to publish it, but in a severely expurgated form. Durrell hesitated, but, stiffened by Henry Miller, decided to publish the text (already cut down from a much longer original draft) in full in Paris. In a preface to the American edition (*The Black Book* is not yet freely published in England) Durrell sees *The Black Book*, for all its crudities, as still very dear to him, because it was the first prose book in which he found his own personal voice.

The outer shape of *The Black Book* is a broadly simple one, that of an inner autobiography enclosed within an outer autobiography. The outer narrator, Lawrence Lucifer, is, like L. G. Darley in *The Alexandria Quartet*, a version of Durrell himself. He moves in a world which is like an extended prose variation, stretching often topographically well beyond inner London, of *The Waste Land*: shabby hotels, grotesque crammer's colleges, excursions into the country, but always a grey half-world of failed artists and defective lovers. The inner narrator, who has disappeared from the immediate scene before Lawrence Lucifer's medi-tations commence, Death Gregory, has left a diary, which Lucifer reads, recounting the agonies of his life. Of gentle or genteel background, Death Gregory has a minor literary talent, of a sub-Paterian sort. Mother-fixated, he has been horribly initiated into sex by a hideous prostitute, but has made a pretty and sick young girl (one thinks of Mürger's Mimi) his mistress and ultimately his wife; he feels for her a tenderness which he is ashamed or unable to express, and also, once he has married her, a social snobbery (for which he is bitterly remorseful) about having married beneath him. Masochistic, he tries to tempt her into having an affair with a sexy gigolo.

When his wife dies, Death Gregory uses his journal to lacerate himself. Lawrence Lucifer, a true artist as Gregory and all the other characters are failed artists, is himself tormented by a love-hate relationship with the English past (too many corpses) and with a young woman who symbolizes for him English pastoral poetry. Lucifer, like Gregory, has had relations with a whore, Hilda, elderly, battered, grotesque, but welcoming and warm-hearted rather than hideous or horrible: a kind of Marie Lloyd figure.

Lucifer's feelings for Hilda are deeply compassionate, though the compassion is expressed in wildly humorous hyperbole and metaphor. Hilda, the whore, is a kind of mother-figure for him; like Gregory, Lucifer perhaps suffers in a subtler way from mother-fixation. He is also fixated on a Madonna figure at his crammer's college, a Frenchwoman, Madame About, dying of cancer of the womb. He gets into murderous rages with his pastoral girl because she is young, fresh, and normal. But the Ur-Mother on whom Lucifer is most fixated is England herself, with her over-powering richness in architecture, landscape, literature, a richness now over-ripe. He feels that the English past stifles him.

Other characters, or perhaps in a Jonsonian sense 'humours', in this narrative include Chamberlain, a hearty Lawrentian life-worshipper, who, however, cannot satisfy his wife: Lucifer sullenly commits adultery with the wife, but feels that he is vicariously committing sodomy with Chamberlain. The wife becomes pregnant, Chamberlain is delighted and gives up his literary ambitions for a safe job in commerce, but Lucifer is sure the child will be still-born. Sadder and stranger variations of sex abound, notably Tancred, a musical composer of some real talent, but a sublimated or repressed homosexual. Tancred takes to a prolonged death-bed after having in late middle age at last sampled both heterosexual and homosexual love-making, and having been equally disgusted with both. Another memorable character is a negro girl to whom Lucifer teaches

Chaucer in the crammer's establishment where he earns his
meagre pittance, remorsefully feeling that he is pumping
ink rather than blood into her good black veins.

Madame About is dying; Hilda is dying; Tancred wants
to die; the negro girl's fine, native, instinctive vitality is
being vitiated. Among so many images of death and decay,
Lawrence Lucifer can have no creed, no philosophy, only
a blind lust for life at any cost. His rage against what he
calls 'the English disease' is a rage against something which
once, say in the Elizabethan period, bred life abundantly
and now seems to breed only frustration and death. *The
Black Book* should be read alongside Auden's *The Orators*:
'What shall we say about England, this country of ours
where nobody is well?' The 'English disease' is Freud's
death-wish. Overtly, and also in the plushy richness of the
prose, there is an image of England as a stiflingly cosy
womb from which Lawrence Lucifer, like the infant
Pantagruel, must somehow, however bloodily and violently,
escape.

A book which has odd affinities with *The Black Book* is
Carlyle's *Sartor Resartus*: the Yea-Saying to life in that
spiritual autobiography (which is marked not only by in-
wardness and poignancy but by a grotesque humour not
unlike Durrell's) is all the more impressive because gloom,
fear, melancholy, a sense of dereliction fit in so much more
naturally with Carlyle's rhetoric, and because the final Yea-
saying is such a bold leap in the dark. Durrell resembles
Carlyle in his grim humour, and his sympathy with the lost;
like Carlyle, he writes never as a satirist but as a dark and
compassionate humorist.

The only character in *The Black Book* whom Lawrence
Lucifer wants at one time to hit is Tancred. He reflects,
however, that Tancred should not be thought of as a person,
as somebody free and therefore responsible for his choices
(and therefore worth hitting, because a blow can be a kind
of argument) but rather as an obsessional monomaniac, as a
Jonsonian 'humour'. One might similarly compare Carlyle's

funny and compassionate handling of the utterly repulsive but infinitely pitiable Égalité Orleans in *The French Revolution*. *The Black Book* is perhaps less important as a novel than as an extraordinarily vivid, exact, and honest document for somebody who might want to write a latter-day version of William James's *The Varieties of Religious Experience*. Durrell did in it an extraordinarily cruel (clinically cruel, cruel to be kind) job of auto-analysis; explored Hell, and perhaps just got out of it; but taught himself, in his journey, compassion.

I am rather alone in the central importance in Durrell's development that I give to *The Black Book*. One of the young lions of the *New Statesman*, Francis Hope, thinks that I 'grossly over-estimate' it. D. J. Enright, a critic and poet very unlike Durrell, but oddly sympathetic to some aspects of his work, thinks that the conscious manipulation of diction and rhythm is a special kind of bad writing. (Just in the same way, Aldous Huxley thought that the prose of George Santayana, so consciously well-written, was immediately recognizable as a special kind of *bad* writing; yet, after all, Santayana had a much profounder *mind* than Huxley.)

Durrell can, in fact, and even in *The Black Book* sometimes does, write plain, direct, unornate prose. For all its spiciness and high colouring, *The Alexandria Quartet*, moves with a much bolder and more rapid rhythm, is nearer the speaking voice. *Tunc* and *Nunquam* are full of purple passages, but of purple passages that deliberately and jokily send themselves up; and the prose of these novels is still bolder, and still more rapid, than *The Alexandria Quartet*. Durrell's great early friend and mentor, Henry Miller, after being bowled over, felt that *The Black Book* was too verbally glutinous, rich, sticky. There is certainly something self-stimulating, self-caressing—about the way that Durrell there fingers his cadences and his climaxes.

Yet if we reject *The Black Book* for such reasons we reject also, I think, automatically, Sir Thomas Browne, Sterne,

Lamb, De Quincey, Landor, Pater, a whole English tradition of ornate prose in which the prose writer is (like a poet) as much concerned with pace, pause, rhythm, speech tunes, an odd and surprising fixing of contrasts of words, phrases, idioms, as with what we call 'content' or 'matter'. Matthew Arnold at a dinner party, as reported by G. W. E. Russell, said: 'Know what you want to say and say it as clearly as possible! That is the sole secret of style.' It quite clearly is not the sole secret of style, though it may be a good working precept for the *Times* leader-writer or the university lecturer. But it is through an obsession with words, their colour, flavour, history, that many writers grope towards a sense of what they 'want to say'. In what one can broadly call writers of ornate or coloured prose, an obsessive concern (and all true artists are in some sense obsessional) with verbal and rhythmical patterning enriches or indeed transforms the 'content' or 'matter', enables, as the stricter rhythms and the more exigent choices about diction of verse do, the writer to achieve a finer, more exact, more flexible and inclusive communication.

Perhaps all art does not aspire, in Pater's sense, to the condition of music; but neither does it aspire to the clear sophistries and flat amenities of a good *Times* leading article or a good *New Statesman* review. It does not aspire towards what Matthew Arnold called the Corinthian style.

The current English case against Durrell's prose is that it is mannerist, too richly and consciously atmospheric and connotational. I am not sure that Durrell is as much a mannerist writer as, say, Hemingway or Gertrude Stein, writers who base their verbal art on a kind of de-connexion, a scrubbing out of traditional connotations, a decreation, and in Gertrude Stein's case, in a work like *Tender Buttons*, on an attempt to desemanticize language, to use individual words like blobs or shapes of colour in an abstract painting. Compared to such writers, who, of course, were experimenting in this way thirty or forty years before him, Durrell is in a sense very old-fashioned. He never sets himself a schema or a project that will exclude spontaneity. He wants to tell a story that will attract a popular as well as a highbrow audience. He is not working in a word laboratory. We should perhaps not be excessively puritan in censuring a writer's under-the-sheet relationships with his main Muse, his crushingly rich maternal and paternal language.

V. THE ALEXANDRIA QUARTET

If *The Black Book* has a special interest both as a kind of spiritual autobiography and as a young man's first finding of his real voice, it is on the four volumes of *The Alexandria Quartet*, *Justine* (1957), *Balthazar* (1958), *Mountolive* (1958), and *Clea* (1960) that Durrell's world-fame mainly rests. All four were published in one volume, with numerous revisions to iron out small inconsistencies in the text, and with a new preface, in 1962. The first three volumes cover roughly the same period of time, and the same series of events, in Alexandria in the period leading up to the Second World War, and the last volume, *Clea*, carries the story forward into the war years, though continuing to develop the three basic themes of art, love, and death, or perhaps art, love, and mysticism.

The narrator, L. G. Darley, like Lawrence Lucifer, has Durrell's own initials (L.G.D., 'Lineaments of Gratified Desire') and a personality rather like the young Durrell's. He is a young man very open to experience, exploring, in a sensitive but often blundering and mistaken way, the possibilities of love and art. He has a Greek mistress, Melissa, who has come to him out of gratitude rather than love (he rescued her from a terrible party where she had been given an aphrodisiac) and he has accepted her out of pity rather than love. Because of a lecture he gives on the great Alexandrian poet Cavafy, he becomes a friend and later, at her initiative, the lover of Justine, the Jewish wife of a rich Coptic businessman, Nessim. A blonde and cool young artist, Clea, has also a sisterly fondness for him, and spends a chaste night with him when he finally leaves Alexandria. It is Justine, however, who mainly obsesses Darley, because of her multi-faceted character, represented symbolically through her looking at herself in a triple mirror, and because of a nymphomania which apparently springs from her having been raped as a young girl by a notorious Alexandrian lecher, Capodistria.

As the novel progresses, Justine becomes more and more nervous, and Darley thinks that her husband Nessim (a highly civilized man, whom Darley likes and respects) may be conspiring to murder him, her, or both of them. Darley goes to a duck-shooting party on Nessim's country estate with great trepidation. Somebody is shot, ostensibly accidentally, but it is (again ostensibly) Capodistria. Justine deserts Nessim and becomes a worker on a kibbutz in Palestine. Pursewarden, an arrogant and sarcastic novelist, whom Darley admires but dislikes, mysteriously commits suicide, leaving Darley some money, which he uses to get Melissa medical treatment. Darley goes for two years to teach in a rather dull Roman Catholic missionary college near Luxor in Upper Egypt. He comes back to Alexandria to see Melissa, who is dying, but she is dead before he has arrived. Melissa has had a child by Nessim, who has turned to her in his loneliness and desperation, and Darley, who (like Durrell himself) is a very generous and obliging person, takes charge of the child and retires to a Greek island where he writes up the whole story in retrospect.

Justine is a very vivid and satisfying novel in itself. In its sequels, *Balthazar* and *Mountolive*, we learn that Darley, though a perfectly trustworthy narrator, had misinterpreted the meaning of all the key events. Justine had never been really in love with Darley, but, if with anybody, with Pursewarden, who had thrust her out of his hotel room shortly before she came to Darley's flat. The marriage of Nessim and Justine was not a love-match (though they are perfectly sexually well adjusted to each other) but a political alliance between the Egyptian Jews and Copts, who are conspiring against the British presence in Egypt and the Near East generally, and smuggling arms (strangely, German Hitlerian arms) into Palestine. Justine's affairs with Darley and Pursewarden are partly genuinely sexual but more fundamentally she is acting as a secret agent, since, in addition to Darley's teaching and Pursewarden's writing, both are British Embassy intelligence agents, Darley a very minor and not very efficient one, Pursewarden a highly placed one.

Pursewarden is not an ideal man for this job, too fundamentally intuitive and indiscreet, and from Melissa, who is one of his many mistresses, he learns that Nessim is at the centre of the conspiracy. He kills himself, having first managed both to warn Nessim and to put the Ambassador, Mountolive, in the picture. Mountolive passes the information on to the more or less puppet Egyptian government. Nessim buys time and life from the head of this, the loathsome Memlek, by lavish bribery, but Memlek has to do something to keep the British (and his own Egyptian rivals and colleagues) quiet and arranges the assassination of Nessim's brother, the hare-lipped fierce and tender country squire, Narouz. One main motive, one might mention in passing, of the Coptic conspiracy is that under the British the Copts have been robbed of the key places in government and administration that they enjoyed under the Turks and under the Egyptian kings of Turkish ancestry. Narouz has been frankly rabble-rousing, which makes his killing explicable.

Mountolive's position is complicated both by the fact that in his youth, sent to Egypt by the Foreign Office to learn Egyptian Arabic, he has been the lover of the mother of Narouz and Nessim, Leila, who might have left Egypt to join him in Europe if she had not been suddenly stricken with confluent small-pox. But his official duties come first to him, and when Leila—an old woman now, drenched in perfume—asks him to protect her sons, he rejects her brutally.

He is punished indirectly by being trapped into visiting a
brothel (Justine has already visited it in a vain search for a
lost child by her earlier marriage) where the children tear
at his clothes, and wound terribly his official image of himself. Mountolive is the lover of Pursewarden's blind sister,
Liza. She has been her brother's lover, but this is not what
worries Mountolive; profoundly conventional, he feels that
it is eccentric for an Ambassador to have a blind wife. One
of the multiple possible motives for Pursewarden's suicide
is to pave the way for this marriage; and after Pursewarden's
death Darley and Liza burn Pursewarden's letters to Liza in
which his genius has perhaps (one thinks of D. H. Lawrence's
letters) expressed itself more fully and spontaneously than
in his novels.

Clea, the coda to this complex story, brings Darley back
to Egypt in the early years of the Second World War, with
Nessim's child by Melissa. Nessim has been, and Justine still
is, under house arrest in one of their country estates, but
Nessim is working his passage by serving in an ambulance
unit in the often heavily bombed docks. He has been
injured, losing an eye and a finger, and Justine herself has
had a slight stroke, leaving her with a drooping eye.
Nessim leaves Darley alone with Justine, and she comes
naked to his bed, stinking of a bottle of perfume which she
has nervously spilt over herself. Darley rejects her (Leila
was similarly stinking of perfume when Mountolive so
brutally rejected her plea for help for Narouz and Nessim).

Darley now discovers that the cool blonde artist, Clea,
not poor little Melissa, not over-eager Justine, is his true
elective affinity: they have an affair which is calm and
idyllic, but its very calmness seems to paralyse both as
artists. She becomes a true artist only when, at a picnic by
the sea, while she is swimming under water, a harpoon is
accidentally (but is anything in Durrell accidental?) fired
and her right hand is transfixed to the sea-floor. Darley
dives, and hacks her free, a doctor, her former lover (whose
wife is a girl whose nose has been eaten away by lupus, but

he has built her a good new grafted-on nose) reconstitutes a partly artificial hand and Clea becomes a really good painter (one thinks of the great painter Renoir, in old age, semi-paralytic, painting with a long brush, the handle as long as a broom handle, strapped to his wrist). True love is not enough. Darley and Clea really love each other when they are at a great distance (she in the South of France, he in a Greek island) working away on their stuff, and sending each other what Auden calls 'long marvellous letters'. The practice of art and the fulfilment of physical love are both 'stages on life's way' to something beyond themselves.

D. J. Enright said in a friendly and courteous review of my longer study of Durrell that my 'very competent' plot summaries revealed how unrelated to real life, real character, Durrell's novels are, how their raw material is mere fantasia. I was surprised at this verdict: I would have thought that somebody like Enright who has worked in Egypt, Singapore, Japan, Thailand, would know how much intrigue, conspiracy, deception, multiple motivation, are a part of Asian life, and how much also Englishmen, in a hot climate, tend to behave sometimes like characters out of the *commedia dell'arte* (like Durrell's great comic character in *The Alexandria Quartet*, Scobie) and how much ,when they are serious, like characters out of Italian opera. The Englishman abroad is not the Englishman at home. I find, in spite of the elements of Arabian night fantasy (but these are usually enclosed stories within the story, not to be taken as 'literally' true, like Capodistria's account of his experiments in creating homunculi), that I can believe both in the people and in what is happening to them in *The Alexandria Quartet*. Angus Wilson has praised Durrell's skill in plot construction, and in one crude sense *The Alexandria Quartet* with its sudden revelations of hitherto unsuspected motivations and purposes at just the right moment to stir and surprise the reader is as neatly constructed as a novel by Simenon or Agatha Christie.

The structural mastery and the basic human plausibility

are worth insisting on because *The Alexandria Quartet* has been a little too much regarded, at least in England, as a triumph mainly of atmospheric bravura writing. For me, and I think for anybody who lived and served in Egypt during the war years, it has the flavour of truth about it: truth is not always drab and consistent and dun-coloured, but sometimes flaring and glaring, astonishing, incongruous. It may be true, nevertheless, that what we remember in the end is less the characters individually than the characters as functions of a landscape or townscape, characters as a function of the whole history of Alexandria, with its traditions of richness and sensuality (Antony and Cleopatra) and of mysticism, magic, quarrelling theologies; the great library, also, and its destruction by the Islamic conquerors. In a crude sense, through sensuality, through art which is the mastering and distancing of sensuality, through love which is one stage further on yet, and through a kind of distancing and spiritualizing of love itself, all the characters are seeking oneness with reality or truth.

There is also Durrell's philosophy, an amateurish one, but very interesting (out of Groddeck and Einstein, one might say, without the intermediation of a professional meta-physician like McTaggart, whose arguments for the un-reality of time, sense, matter, and for reality as finally a community of spirits timelessly knowing and loving each other, Durrell, like Yeats, who spoke of 'profound McTaggart', might find very rewarding).

Durrell can occasionally create a very evil character, like the abominable Memlek, but he is not a social moralist as, I suppose, most of the greater English novelists are. Neither is he a 'naturalist' for though he sees all his characters as functions of a landscape, of a long and deeply-rooted local history, still he gives all of them the freedom of apparently arbitrary choice. They reject, accept, kill themselves, come together or leave each other, in a way that seems spon-taneously 'natural' but not 'naturalistic'. They are also not seen as separate or self-contained characters. Melissa, inspiring compassion, Justine, inspiring passion. Clea, inspiring desire and companionship, what Durrell calls 'loving-kindness', are three aspects of womanhood. Narouz, the fierce country squire, and Nessim, the almost over-civilized business man, brothers who love and perhaps secretly envy each other, are two incomplete aspects of one possible person. Darley and Pursewarden are the artist in formation, and the formed artist passing beyond art.

Every relationship is a way of learning, and in the end of passing beyond, a new role. Alexandria, the true heroine of this novel, manifests itself in many selves, in many roles, but is in the end the single source: more real, more potent than her various manifestations. She hurts, she can kill, but she also resurrects. Justine, at first a kind of goddess, then a clever and ruthless Levantine conspirator, then a broken and rejected woman, is resurrected in the end, smartly dressed, walking along the Alexandria *trottoir*, on her high heels, arm in arm, dreaming of newer and grander con-spiracies—it is only danger and conspiracy that sparks off her sexual eagerness!—with the abominable Memlek.

VI. *TUNC* AND *NUNQUAM*

Durrell makes a major effort in fiction only at comparatively rare intervals. The 1960s were a fairly fallow period. In 1963 he published his play *An Irish Faustus*, in 1965 another verse play *Acte*. I have spoken of these in the introductory section: both acted in Germany, *Faustus* with considerable success (it went into repertoire), they aroused no critical interest at all in England; and the performance, ten years after its publica-tion, of his first play *Sappho* (the richest of the three in purely poetic language, though the least tightly constructed as a drama) at the Edinburgh Festival of 1960 evoked only tepid or sometimes actively hostile responses from the critics. A new volume of Antrobus stories, Wodehousian pictures of Embassy life in the Balkans, *Sauve Qui Peut*, published in

1966, was found only mildly amusing, and a critic in a good critical journal, Ian Hamilton's *The Review*, found Durrell's one new volume of poems of the 1960s, *The Ikons*, tasteful but rather dead, too reminiscent of Walter Savage Landor.

His most ambitious book of the 1960s was *Tunc*, published in 1968, and followed in 1970 by its sequel *Nunquam*. *Tunc* sold, as Durrell always sells, remarkably well, but tended to puzzle and bewilder English critics. There were some superficial resemblances to *The Alexandria Quartet*, as also to *The Black Book*: the handling of prose was, it seems to me, free from the congestion of *The Black Book* and from the sometimes too conscious 'fine writing' even of the much more freely handled *Alexandria Quartet*; but the characters were, as Durrell admitted himself, much more 'puppets': the scene ranged from Athens to Constantinople to London to Paris and, in the sequel *Nunquam*, to Switzerland, to Constantinople, and back to London, but the evocation of place, though often brilliant, was much more rapid and sketchy. There was no attempt in the story-line at surface plausibility. One might have been reminded, indeed, in the plot-line, of a thriller by Dennis Wheatley. Durrell was writing not a novel, even in the sense in which *The Alexandria Quartet* for all its bravura extravagances is a novel rather than a romance, but a philosophic romance, such as Godwin's *Caleb Williams* or Mary Shelley's *Frankenstein*. Appealing for once simultaneously to his popular and sophisticated audiences, he constructed a story which is full of thrills, horror, and suspense; but, as with Godwin and Mary Shelley, the Gothick romance appealed to him mainly as a vehicle for the expression of ideas.

An intelligent reviewer in *The Times Literary Supplement* noted this fact, but felt that the choice or use of ideas was in a sense 'opportunistic'. I think such a remark did an injustice to Durrell's engagement and sincerity. He believes, with Spengler, that we have now reached, in Western Europe, America, and perhaps all over the world, a stage which should not be called 'culture' but rather 'civilization'.

Our lives no longer grow out of an organic local culture, as in a sense the lives of the characters in *The Alexandria Quartet* grew, but out of McLuhan's 'global village', the world of instant mass communication; and our lives tend to be shaped and channelled by great international consortia, like The Firm in Durrell's double-decker, over which we have little democratic control, and from which we find it hard to escape once we have signed our contracts with them (there is a strong reminiscence of the Faustus story here).

All this is reminiscent of Orwell's *1984* and Huxley's *Brave New World*. What is original in Durrell's approach is the idea that individual attempts to escape from The Firm, from the bureaucratic and mass communications society, are futile: it is better, in the end, to co-operate with The Firm and to inspire it with a spirit of benevolence and freedom. No individual can be free, unless all men are free; the hero, Felix Charlock, caught up in The Firm, and then futilely attempting to escape from it, and then cunningly dodging brainwashing in a Swiss sanatorium, in the end after the death of Julian (the head of The Firm, at first Charlock's ruthless enemy, and then his friend) takes The Firm over, and arranges to have all the microfilmed contracts, which bind its slaves to it, burned. He remains, however, rather sceptical. Freedom is a very difficult thing to choose and members of The Firm may wish to continue to work for it, even after they are not in danger of death if they refuse. But if the whole spirit of The Firm has changed, this eventuality may be less disastrous than it seems.

It would be pointless to summarize the thrilling, intricate, but deliberately highly improbable plot of *Aut Tunc Aut Nunquam* here. One may merely state that Durrell, here as elsewhere always highly professional, knows exactly what he is doing, though what he is doing may disconcert many of his earlier admirers. Incidents and descriptions are deliberately garish and shocking, there is a lot of use of what one might describe as poster-colour: Durrell, in an age which is growingly non-literary, is deliberately competing for attention with, say, pop art and horror comics. If the passages one remembers most in *The Alexandria Quartet* are, so to say, erotic and lyrical, the typical note of *Aut Tunc Aut Nunquam* is macabre and grotesque (there are some fine erotic and lyrical passages in *Aut Tunc Aut Nunquam*, just as there are some fine macabre and grotesque passages in *The Alexandria Quartet*: but the proportions have shifted).

The most illuminating comment on the general form of *Tunc* and *Nunquam* that I have read is by Northrop Frye, who, in his *Anatomy of Criticism*, published in 1957, could not possibly have had these two still unwritten and un-conceived novels in mind, but might almost have been foreseeing them:

> The essential difference between novel and romance lies in the concept of characterization. The romancer does not attempt to create 'real people' so much as stylized figures which expand into psychological archetypes. It is in the romance that we find Jung's libido, anima, and shadow reflected in the hero, heroine, and villain respectively. That is why the romance so often radiates a glow of subjective intensity that the novel lacks, and why a suggestion of allegory is always creeping round its fringes.

Charlock, Benedicta, and Julian fit the roles of libido, anima, and shadow exactly, and Charlock's reconciliation with Julian and inheriting of, and transforming of, Julian's post in the Firm is in line with Jung's psychology of integra-tion. On the other hand the 'suggestion of allegory . . . always creeping round its fringes' is what has irritated readers who like their allegory clear-cut, as in *The Pilgrim's Progress* or *Gulliver's Travels*. Frye notes that 'certain elements of character are revealed in the romance which make it naturally a more revolutionary form than the novel'. The archetypal figures in *Tunc* and *Nunquam*, like archetypal figures in dreams, both break many taboos and make us aware of primeval taboos we had forgotten. The double-decker story is much less visual than any previous work of fiction of Durrell's and makes more use—in its prose technique and, in a sense, even in its plot—of the auditory imagination, puns, ambiguous allusions, emblematic names, the idea of auditory hallucination. Consciously, the romance is an allegory about a somewhat ambiguous concept of 'civilization'—the decay of culture, the growth of international bureaucracy, the death of religion. Unconsciously, it may be a projection of some inner stress, some near-breakdown, which its author may have at least imagined and some of its readers may have suffered; that would help to give the double-decker its power for those readers, and I am one, who find it powerful.

There is plenty of comedy in both works but the comedy in *Aut Tunc Aut Nunquam* is much nearer farce, or barrack-room bawdry, and has also an agreeable quality of self-parody: as when Felix Charlock, the hero, quotes 'our most distinguished modern poet' and an asterisk refers us in a footnote to the name of Lawrence Durrell. I think reviewers, ever-mindful of the 'high seriousness' of the novel as a form, have done less than justice, on the whole, to the verve and high spirits of *Tunc* and *Nunquam*. If the deeper meaning of *The Alexandria Quartet* is a mystical or transcendental meaning, the deeper meaning of *Aut Tunc Aut Nunquam* is a social-philosophical one. It seems to me a serious and sane meaning: as a university teacher, for instance, I would agree with Durrell that what we need is a general spirit of freedom in our institutions, a greater flexibility and generosity, rather than individual rejection of, or rebellion against, the idea of an institution as such. Durrell, I think, has never written more freshly and entertainingly than in these two books. As he said at his press conference on *Nunquam*, when he looks at the world around us, he is filled with grim forebodings, but deeper than that is an innate optimism, a Yea-saying to Life itself. It is always now or never, *aut tunc aut nunquam*, for every human soul. We are not chessmen or items in a census or a sociological survey. At any moment, we may say 'Yes', and be free.

Tempted very much by some aspects of his life and character, his youthful wish to be a best-seller, by his official posts with Embassies, The British Council, and government Information Services, by his sheer natural amenity and good manners, to be a conformist, Durrell has again and again made a sideways leap into the unexpected, the disturbingly new, into freedom. Quite apart from the permanent value of his best writing, I think his career, his readiness to accept new situations, new places, new jobs, to be *serviable*, and his other readiness to sweat at creative freedom when it is offered to him, hold out a valuable lesson, an exemplary lesson, to the younger writers of today. He has never stopped trying and learning. He has never thought the world owed him a living; but the world has been his oyster, which he has opened, not like Ancient Pistol with his sword, but with his pen.

LAWRENCE DURRELL

A Select Bibliography

(Place of publication London, unless stated otherwise)

Bibliography:

LAWRENCE DURRELL: A Checklist, compiled by R. A. Potter and B. Whiting; Los Angeles (1961).

LAWRENCE DURRELL: A Study, by G. S. Fraser (1968)

—contains a bibliography by A. G. Thomas which includes books, translations, prefaces and miscellaneous articles by and about Durrell, as well as lists of recordings and television appearances.

Collected and Selected Works:

SELECTED POEMS (1956)

—an enlarged paperback edition was issued in 1964 as *Selected Poems, 1953–63*.

COLLECTED POEMS (1960).

THE ALEXANDRIA QUARTET: Justine, Balthazar, Mountolive, Clea (1962). *Fiction*

—the four novels in one volume, with numerous revisions in the text and a new preface.

Separate Works:

TEN POEMS (1932).

BALLADE OF SLOW DECAY (1932).

TRANSITION (1934). *Poems*

PIED PIPER OF LOVERS (1935). *Fiction*

PANIC SPRING (1937). *Fiction*

—published under the pseudonym Charles Norden.

THE BLACK BOOK; Paris (1938). *Fiction*

A PRIVATE COUNTRY (1943). *Poems*

PROSPERO'S CELL: A Guide to the Landscape and Manners of the Island of Corcyra (1945).

ZERO, AND ASYLUM IN THE SNOW: Two Excursions into Reality; privately printed, Rhodes (1946).

CITIES, PLAINS AND PEOPLE (1946). *Poems*

CEFALÛ (1947). *Fiction*

—republished in 1958, with minor revisions, as *The Dark Labyrinth*.

ON SEEMING TO PRESUME (1948). *Poems*

SAPPHO: a Play in Verse (1950).

DEUS LOCI: a Poem; Ischia (1950).

KEY TO MODERN POETRY (1952). *Criticism*

REFLECTIONS ON A MARINE VENUS: A Companion to the Landscape of Rhodes (1953).

THE TREE OF IDLENESS, and other poems (1955).

PRIVATE DRAFTS; privately printed, Nicosia (1955). *Poems*

SELECTED POEMS (1956)

—an enlarged paperback edition was issued in 1964 as *Selected Poems, 1953–63*.

BITTER LEMONS (1957). *Travel*

ESPRIT DE CORPS: Sketches from Diplomatic Life (1957). *Stories*

JUSTINE (1957). *Fiction*

WHITE EAGLES OVER SERBIA (1957). *Fiction*

BALTHAZAR (1958). *Fiction*

MOUNTOLIVE (1958). *Fiction*

STIFF UPPER LIP: Life Among the Diplomats (1958). *Stories*

—illustrated by Nicolas Bentley.

ART AND OUTRAGE: A Correspondence about Henry Miller between Alfred Perlès and Lawrence Durrell, with an intermission by Henry Miller (1959).

CLEA (1960). *Fiction*

BECCAFICO; Montpellier, Leghorn (1963).

LAWRENCE DURRELL—HENRY MILLER: A Private Correspondence, ed. G. Wickes (1963). *Literary and philosophic correspondence*

AN IRISH FAUSTUS: a Morality in Nine Scenes (1963). *Verse Play*

ACTE (1964). *Verse Play*

SAUVE QUI PEUT (1966). *Stories*

THE IKONS, and other poems (1966).

TUNC (1968). *Fiction*

SPIRIT OF PLACE: Letters and Essays on Travel, ed. A. G. Thomas (1969).

NUNQUAM (1970). *Fiction*

—a sequel to *Tunc*.

Some Biographical and Critical Studies:

LEAVES IN THE STORM: a Book of Diaries, ed. S. Schimanski and H. Treece (1947)

—contains 'Athens in Spring (Katsimbalis and Durrell)' by Sir J. Waller.

THE PENGUIN BOOK OF CONTEMPORARY VERSE, ed. K. Allott (1950)
—contains a biocritical sketch by the editor, introducing his selection from Durrell's poems.

MY FAMILY AND OTHER ANIMALS, by G. Durrell (1956)
—contains sketches by his brother of Lawrence Durrell as a young man in Corfu.

MY FRIEND LAWRENCE DURRELL, by A. Perlès (1961).

THE WORLD OF LAWRENCE DURRELL, ed. H. T. Moore; Carbondale (1962).

LAWRENCE DURRELL, by J. Unterecker; New York (1964).

LAWRENCE DURRELL, by J. A. Weigel; New York (1965).

LAWRENCE DURRELL: A Study, by G. S. Fraser, with a bibliography by A. G. Thomas (1968).

Note: An unpublished dissertation entitled *Lawrence Durrell: Time in 'The Alexandria Quartet'*, by Chan Soo Ping was submitted in 1969 to the Department of English in The University of Malaya for the degree of MA. This contains both the clearest elucidation of Durrell's space-time theories and the closest and most elegant structural analysis of *The Alexandria Quartet* yet written.

WRITERS AND THEIR WORK

General Surveys:

THE DETECTIVE STORY IN BRITAIN :
Julian Symons
THE ENGLISH BIBLE : Donald Coggan
ENGLISH VERSE EPIGRAM :
G. Rostrevor Hamilton
ENGLISH HYMNS : A. Pollard
ENGLISH MARITIME WRITING :
Hakluyt to Cook: Oliver Warner
THE ENGLISH SHORT STORY I : & II :
T. O. Beachcroft
THE ENGLISH SONNET : P. Cruttwell
ENGLISH SERMONS : Arthur Pollard
ENGLISH TRAVELLERS IN THE
NEAR EAST : Robin Fedden
THREE WOMEN DIARISTS : M. Willy

Sixteenth Century and Earlier:

FRANCIS BACON : J. Max Patrick
BEAUMONT & FLETCHER : Ian Fletcher
CHAUCER : Nevill Coghill
GOWER & LYDGATE : Derek Pearsall
RICHARD HOOKER : A. Pollard
THOMAS KYD : Philip Edwards
LANGLAND : Nevill Coghill
LYLY & PEELE : G. K. Hunter
MALORY : M. C. Bradbrook
MARLOWE : Philip Henderson
SIR THOMAS MORE : E. E. Reynolds
RALEGH : Agnes Latham
SIDNEY : Kenneth Muir
SKELTON : Peter Green
SPENSER : Rosemary Freeman
THREE 14TH-CENTURY ENGLISH
MYSTICS : Phyllis Hodgson
TWO SCOTS CHAUCERIANS :
H. Harvey Wood
WYATT : Sergio Baldi

Seventeenth Century:

SIR THOMAS BROWNE : Peter Green
BUNYAN : Henri Talon
CAVALIER POETS : Robin Skelton
CONGREVE : Bonamy Dobrée
DONNE : F. Kermode
DRYDEN : Bonamy Dobrée
ENGLISH DIARISTS :
Evelyn and Pepys: M. Willy
FARQUHAR : A. J. Farmer
JOHN FORD : Clifford Leech
GEORGE HERBERT : T. S. Eliot
HERRICK : John Press
HOBBES : T. E. Jessop
BEN JONSON : J. B. Bamborough
LOCKE : Maurice Cranston
ANDREW MARVELL : John Press
MILTON : E. M. W. Tillyard

RESTORATION COURT POETS :
V. de S. Pinto
SHAKESPEARE : C. J. Sisson
CHRONICLES : Clifford Leech
EARLY COMEDIES : Derek Traversi
LATER COMEDIES : G. K. Hunter
FINAL PLAYS : F. Kermode
HISTORIES : L. C. Knights
POEMS : F. T. Prince
PROBLEM PLAYS : Peter Ure
ROMAN PLAYS : T. J. B. Spencer
GREAT TRAGEDIES : Kenneth Muir
THREE METAPHYSICAL POETS :
Margaret Willy
IZAAK WALTON : Margaret Bottrall
WEBSTER : Ian Scott-Kilvert
WYCHERLEY : P. F. Vernon

Eighteenth Century:

BERKELEY : T. E. Jessop
BLAKE : Kathleen Raine
BOSWELL : P. A. W. Collins
BURKE : T. E. Utley
BURNS : David Daiches
WM. COLLINS : Oswald Doughty
COWPER : N. Nicholson
CRABBE : R. L. Brett
DEFOE : J. R. Sutherland
FIELDING : John Butt
GAY : Oliver Warner
GIBBON : C. V. Wedgwood
GOLDSMITH : A. Norman Jeffares
GRAY : R. W. Ketton-Cremer
HUME : Montgomery Belgion
JOHNSON : S. C. Roberts
POPE : Ian Jack
RICHARDSON : R. F. Brissenden
SHERIDAN : W. A. Darlington
CHRISTOPHER SMART : G. Grigson
SMOLLETT : Laurence Brander
STEELE, ADDISON : A. R. Humphreys
STERNE : D. W. Jefferson
SWIFT : J. Middleton Murry
SIR JOHN VANBRUGH : Bernard Harris
HORACE WALPOLE : Hugh Honour

Nineteenth Century:

MATTHEW ARNOLD : Kenneth Allott
JANE AUSTEN : S. Townsend Warner
BAGEHOT : N. St John-Stevas
THE BRONTË SISTERS : P. Bentley
BROWNING : John Bryson
E. B. BROWNING : Alethea Hayter
SAMUEL BUTLER : G. D. H. Cole
BYRON : Bernard Blackstone
CARLYLE : David Gascoyne
LEWIS CARROLL : Derek Hudson

CLOUGH: Isobel Armstrong
COLERIDGE: Kathleen Raine
CREEVEY & GREVILLE: J. Richardson
DE QUINCEY: Hugh Sykes Davies
DICKENS: K. J. Fielding
  EARLY NOVELS: T. Blount
  LATER NOVELS: B. Hardy
DISRAELI: Paul Bloomfield
GEORGE ELIOT: Lettice Cooper
FERRIER & GALT: W. M. Parker
FITZGERALD: Joanna Richardson
MRS. GASKELL: Miriam Allott
GISSING: A. C. Ward
THOMAS HARDY: R. A. Scott-James
          and C. Day Lewis
HAZLITT: J. B. Priestley
HOOD: Laurence Brander
G. M. HOPKINS: Geoffrey Grigson
T. H. HUXLEY: William Irvine
KEATS: Edmund Blunden
LAMB: Edmund Blunden
LANDOR: G. Rostrevor Hamilton
EDWARD LEAR: Joanna Richardson
MACAULAY: G. R. Potter
MEREDITH: Phyllis Bartlett
JOHN STUART MILL: M. Cranston
WILLIAM MORRIS: P. Henderson
NEWMAN: J. M. Cameron
PATER: Iain Fletcher
PEACOCK: J. I. M. Stewart
ROSSETTI: Oswald Doughty
CHRISTINA ROSSETTI: G. Battiscombe
RUSKIN: Peter Quennell
SIR WALTER SCOTT: Ian Jack
SHELLEY: G. M. Matthews
SOUTHEY: Geoffrey Carnall
R. L. STEVENSON: G. B. Stern
SWINBURNE: H. J. C. Grierson
TENNYSON: F. L. Lucas
THACKERAY: Laurence Brander
FRANCIS THOMPSON: P. Butter
TROLLOPE: Hugh Sykes Davies
OSCAR WILDE: James Laver
WORDSWORTH: Helen Darbishire

Twentieth Century:
CHINUA ACHEBE: A. Ravenscroft
W. H. AUDEN: Richard Hoggart
HILAIRE BELLOC: Renée Haynes
ARNOLD BENNETT: F. Swinnerton
EDMUND BLUNDEN: Alec M. Hardie
ELIZABETH BOWEN: Jocelyn Brooke
ROBERT BRIDGES: J. Sparrow
ROY CAMPBELL: David Wright
JOYCE CARY: Walter Allen
G. K. CHESTERTON: C. Hollis
WINSTON CHURCHILL: John Connell
R. G. COLLINGWOOD: E.W.F. Tomlin
I. COMPTON-BURNETT: P. H. Johnson

JOSEPH CONRAD: Oliver Warner
WALTER DE LA MARE: K. Hopkins
NORMAN DOUGLAS: Ian Greenlees
T. S. ELIOT: M. C. Bradbrook
FIRBANK & BETJEMAN: J. Brooke
FORD MADOX FORD: Kenneth Young
E. M. FORSTER: Rex Warner
CHRISTOPHER FRY: Derek Stanford
JOHN GALSWORTHY: R. H. Mottram
WM. GOLDING: Clive Pemberton
ROBERT GRAVES: M. Seymour-Smith
GRAHAM GREENE: Francis Wyndham
L. P. HARTLEY & ANTHONY POWELL:
    P. Bloomfield and B. Bergonzi
A. E. HOUSMAN: Ian Scott-Kilvert
ALDOUS HUXLEY: Jocelyn Brooke
HENRY JAMES: Michael Swan
PAMELA HANSFORD JOHNSON:
               Isabel Quigly
JAMES JOYCE: J. I. M. Stewart
RUDYARD KIPLING: Bonamy Dobrée
D. H. LAWRENCE: Kenneth Young
C. DAY LEWIS: Clifford Dyment
WYNDHAM LEWIS: E. W. F. Tomlin
COMPTON MACKENZIE: K. Young
LOUIS MACNEICE: John Press
KATHERINE MANSFIELD: Ian Gordon
JOHN MASEFIELD: L. A. G. Strong
SOMERSET MAUGHAM: J. Brophy
GEORGE MOORE: A. Norman Jeffares
EDWIN MUIR: J. C. Hall
J. MIDDLETON MURRY: Philip Mairet
SEAN O'CASEY: W. A. Armstrong
GEORGE ORWELL: Tom Hopkinson
POETS OF 1939-45 WAR: R. N. Currey
POWYS BROTHERS: R. C. Churchill
J. B. PRIESTLEY: Ivor Brown
HERBERT READ: Francis Berry
FOUR REALIST NOVELISTS: V. Brome
BERNARD SHAW: A. C. Ward
EDITH SITWELL: John Lehmann
OSBERT SITWELL: Roger Fulford
KENNETH SLESSOR: C. Semmler
C. P. SNOW: William Cooper
STRACHEY: R. A. Scott-James
SYNGE & LADY GREGORY: E. Coxhead
DYLAN THOMAS: G. S. Fraser
EDWARD THOMAS: Vernon Scannell
G. M. TREVELYAN: J. H. Plumb
WAR POETS: 1914-18: E. Blunden
EVELYN WAUGH: Christopher Hollis
H. G. WELLS: Montgomery Belgion
PATRICK WHITE: R. F. Brissenden
CHARLES WILLIAMS: J. Heath-Stubbs
ANGUS WILSON: K. W. Gransden
VIRGINIA WOOLF: B. Blackstone
W. B. YEATS: G. S. Fraser
ANDREW YOUNG & R. S. THOMAS:
         L. Clark and R. G. Thomas